PICTURING CHINESE

PICTURING CHINESE

ThunderStone Books
Las Vegas, Nevada

Text © Thunderstone Books, 2014
Illustrations © Bennett Noorda, 2014

This book may not be reproduced in whole or in part, in any form or by any means, electronic or mechanical, including photocopying, recording, or by any information storage and retrieval system now known or hereafter invented, without written permission from the publisher.

978-1-63411-000-6 (ISBN 13)

About This Book

Picturing Chinese will expose you to some of the most common pictographic Chinese characters. These characters were created to look like the objects they represent which is why this book uses pictures to help you remember these characters. In addition, these pictographic characters are often used as radicals which means you will come across them as pieces of other characters. Knowing the basic Chinese characters from *Picturing Chinese* will help you better understand many other characters as you continue to learn to read and write Chinese.

There are 12 characters explained in this book. For each character you will learn a brief history of the character and how it is used in combination with other characters or as a radical piece within certain characters. Use the accompanying pictures as visual reminders for keeping these characters in your memory.

About Chinese Characters

Traditionally, there are six ways in which Chinese characters are created. Although we don't know the precise history of each character, and the principles often overlap, it provides a helpful framework for understanding the Chinese writing system.

First, we have *pictograms*. These characters have evolved from rough pictures representing real-world objects. This book looks at these characters, as they are among the oldest characters and are often used as radicals, forming portions of other characters.

Similar to pictograms are *ideograms*. Instead of objects, ideograms represent concepts or ideas. The number three, for instance, is represented by the character 三. It is not a pictogram of three particular items, but rather an ideogram of the concept of three.

Next we have *compound ideographs*. By combining multiple pictographic or ideographic characters, a new idea is expressed. A man 人 near a tree 木 represents rest, from the idea of a man resting in the shade of a tree.

Many characters are also formed via *phonetic loan*, in which an existing character is borrowed to express something with a similar sound. In many cases, the original character is later modified to avoid confusion. The character 少 originally represented sand but was later borrowed to mean few, and the original character was edited by adding the water radical to become 沙.

The most common type of characters are *phono-semantic* or *radical-phonetic* characters. In these characters, one radical—meaning one character used as a portion of another or a "building block" of sorts—is used to express the meaning, and another to provide the pronunciation. Remember, however, that the pronunciation may only be similar, and have changed over thousands of years. As an example, we find many characters with the phonetic 长, said "cháng" or "zhǎng." Characters such as 张, 帐, 怅 and 伥 all use another radical to clarify meaning and use 长 to provide pronunciation.

Finally, there are a small number of characters believed to be *derivative cognates*. In these cases, characters have the same root but split into different meanings and different characters. This category is not well understood.

As you begin to read and write Chinese characters, pay attention to the basic building blocks. This book will introduce you to a few common ones, but you will find many more in your own study and practice. 加油!

—Robert Noorda

子 zi

子 symbolizes a young child. It can be used together with other characters to express words involving children such as 儿子, meaning *son*. It can also be used as a radical, combined with other characters to form entirely new ones. For instance, a woman 女 together with her child 子 forms the common character 好, meaning *good*.

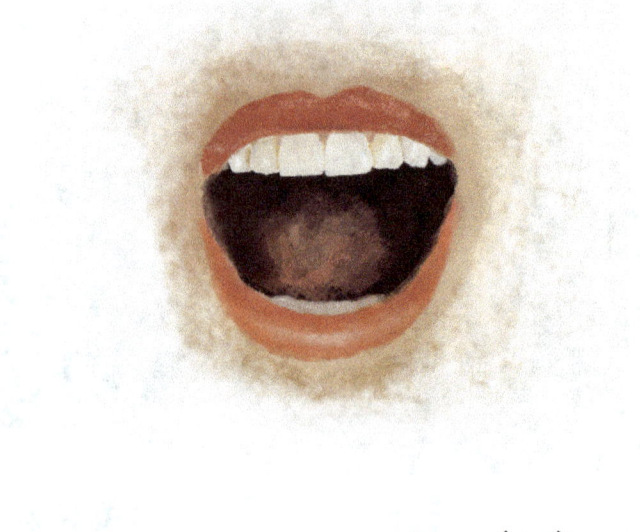

口 kǒu

This character, 口, represents an open mouth. It is commonly used as a radical to indicate sound. For example, the character 哈 takes the sound of 合 and adds the 口 radical to mean the sound of laughter, hā. Similarly, the character 黑 is said hēi and means black. 嘿 is used to express the English word "hey", used to get attention, as in, "Hey you!"

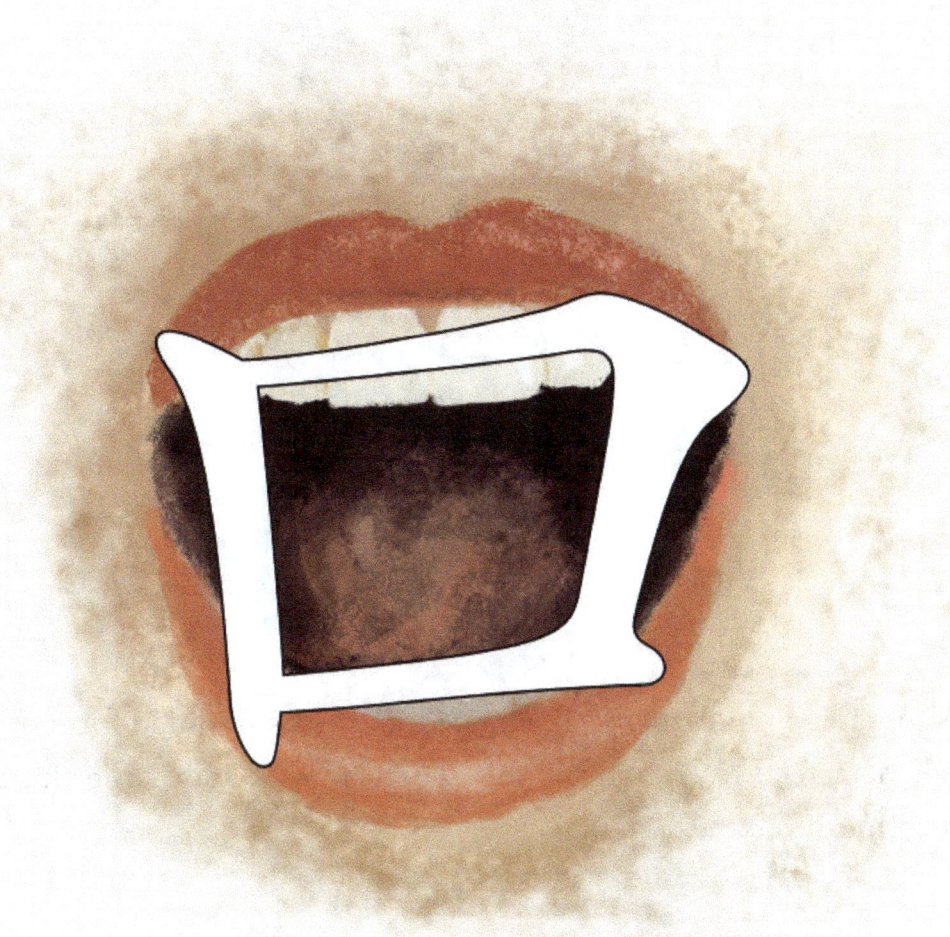

门   mén

门 is a pictographic representation of a door, and the simplified form of the traditional character 門. Combining this character with another in this book creates 门口, which means *doorway*.

火 huǒ

火 represents *fire* or *flame*. When combined with other characters it can take several forms. Sometimes it keeps the same basic form, such as in the first radical in both characters 爆炸, meaning *explode*. In other characters, 火 is represented by four dots ⺣ at the bottom of the character, as in 热, meaning *hot*.

月　yuè

An image of the moon, 月 can be used with another character from this book, 日, meaning *sun*. Together, they form 明, meaning *bright* or *clear*. 月 is also used to mean *month*, similar to how the English word is based on *moon* as well.

日 rì

日 comes from an image of the sun. It is used in the character 旦 to represent the sun coming over the horizon, or *dawn*. This character is also commonly used to mean *day* or *date*.

雨 yǔ

This character represents falling raindrops. It can be used as a radical to form the character 雪, meaning *snow* or 雯, meaning *colorful clouds*.

刂 dāo

刀 is an image of a knife, particularly a one-sided blade. The radical form is often abbreviated to 刂, which is shown in the image on the right. For instance, combining 刀 with the character for *grain* 禾 becomes 利, meaning *profit* or *advantage*, from the idea of harvesting grain with a knife.

山 shān

山 is a pictograph of a mountain. It can be used similarly to the word *mount* in English, as in Mount Everest. Two mountains together led to the character 出, representing a mountain pass, now used to mean *exit*.

人   rén

An image of a man walking, this character means *person*. It is used as a radical in many characters that involve people, such as the pronouns 你 *you* and 他 *he*.

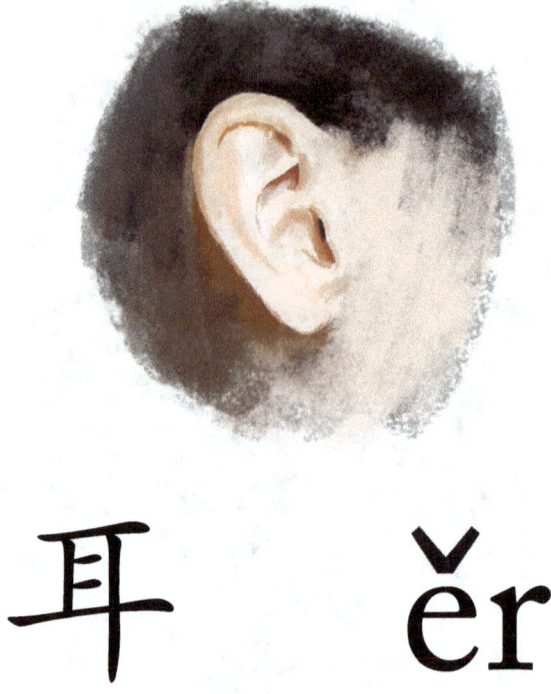

耳 ěr

This character was originally a pictogram of an ear. One example is the word 木耳. Combining the characters tree and ear creates the character for a type of fungus that commonly grows on trees. This fungus is eaten in many parts of China.

The character 目 is an eye. It has been rotated from its original form, so in the picture on the right, the character has been placed horizontally. Common characters with this radical inlcude 盲, meaning *blind*, and 看, the verb *to see*.

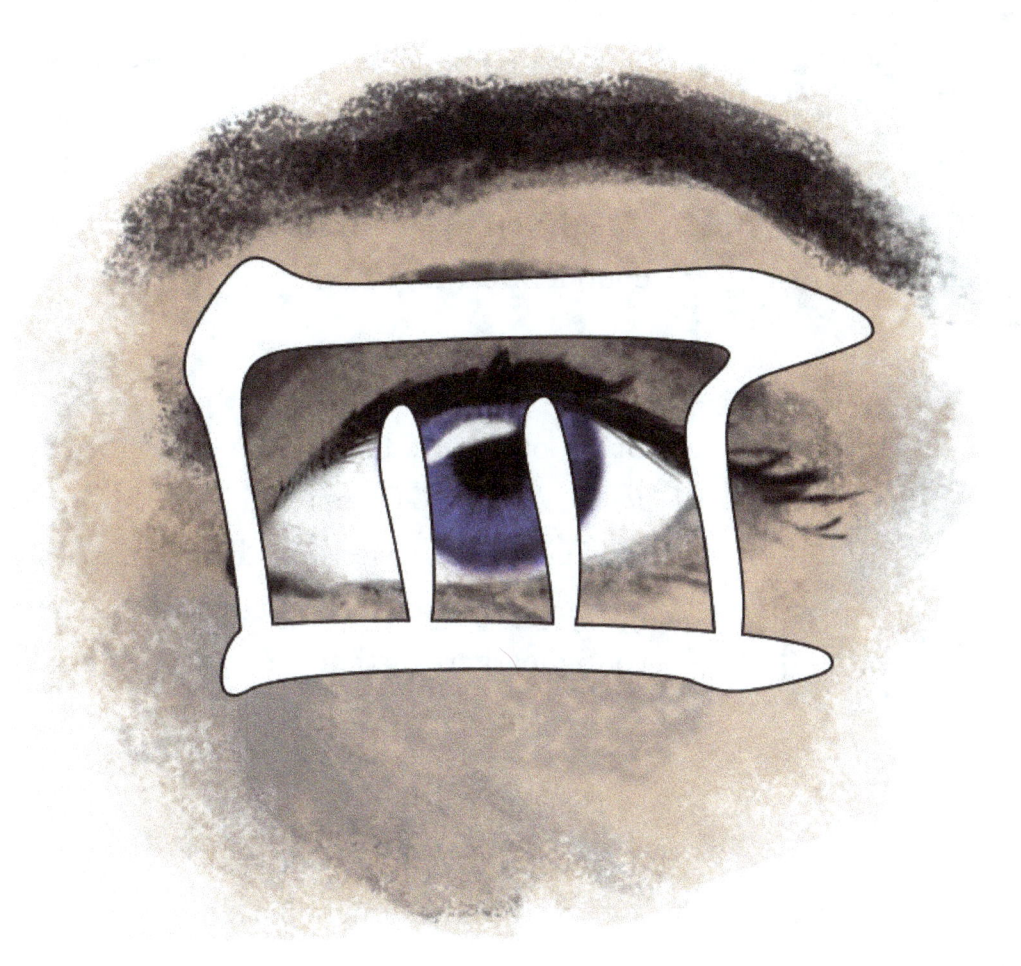

Looking to further your Chinese language learning?

In this first book of Sun Wukong's adventures, join him as he becomes king of the monkeys and goes on a quest to gain his magical powers. Will he be able to master his skills so he can conquer death?

Based on the traditional Chinese story of *Journey to the West*, this bilingual children's book in Mandarin Chinese and English uses simple language and beautiful illustrations to help young learners further their language skills.

Visit us online at www.thunderstonebooks.com

www.ingramcontent.com/pod-product-compliance
Lightning Source LLC
Chambersburg PA
CBHW051354070526
44584CB00025B/3766